Under The Cerulean Skies

Verses on Nature, Nostalgia and Tender Moments

Vaishnavi Vanamali

BookLeaf Publishing

India | USA | UK

Made with ❤ on the BookLeaf Publishing Platform
www.bookleafpub.in
www.bookleafpub.com

Dedication

To **Dad** and **Mom**,

Thank you for always believing in me, for your love, your sacrifices, and for being my biggest supporters.

This is for you.

Preface

This book is a collection of poems that have been written over the years, starting when I was 19. Through the years, I've gathered these pieces - each one capturing moments, memories, and snippets from walks under the sky, silent conversations, and embracing the little things that often go unnoticed.

These poems aren't complicated, they are honest. Each piece is a reflection - sometimes simple, sometimes layered of moments that moved me, made me pause, or helped me see the world a little differently.

I hope as you read, you find pieces of yourself in these words - comfort in the familiar, curiosity in the unknown, and a reminder that beauty often lives in the ordinary.

Thank you for taking the time to step into my world, one poem at a time.

Acknowledgements

First and foremost, I want to express my deepest gratitude to *Venkat* ~ my soulmate, my partner in every sense. You've been my biggest cheerleader, and I'm truly grateful for your endless love, patience and support.

I extend my deepest thanks to *Book Leaf Publishing* for giving me the platform to bring my first book to life.

To my *friends and mentors* - Thank you for your encouragement, kind words and belief in me.

And to *nature*, the ever - present muse, thank you for teaching me to see the magic in the smallest of things, for showing me that love resides in every leaf, every sky, and every fleeting moment.

February

The sky is wrapped in a misty hue,
As frozen whispers linger through.
The silent snow, though draped with grace,
Is urged to melt, to leave its place.

The northern winds still softly sigh,
Yet golden rays now warm the sky.
The frost that once had ruled the land,
Now yields beneath the sun's command.

The coldness lingers in the air,
But love is felt in moments rare.
Soft whispers travel through the trees,
As hearts are stirred by gentle breeze.

Confessions drift like snow so light,
Melting into days more bright.
The skies turn soft, the winds now sing,
Of blossoms near and hope they bring.

A month of love, a heart's embrace,
Where warmth is found in every space.
The winds will shift, the sun will rise,
And summer's dream will kiss the skies.

Whisper

Before the screens took up our gaze,
We lived in brighter, freer days.
Chalk on streets and rain-drenched feet,
Evenings echoed with laughter sweet.

School bags heavy, hearts so light,
Cartoons sharp at five each night.
Game CDs, marbles, spinning tops,
Ice cream bells and candy shops.

Handwritten notes in class would fly,
Friendship bands we'd proudly tie.
No selfies, just those photo rolls,
That captured joy in honest souls.

Now memories dance like fireflies,
Flickering soft in twilight skies.
With every laugh, a story spun,
In the pages of youth, we'd always run.

Lusara

She melts into sleep on my shoulder bare,
A sleepy little hug, without a care.

She giggles when she sees a toy,
Her spirit leaps with unfiltered joy.

Her smile heals what words cannot fix,
A magic found in no grown-up tricks.

She twirls through fields of dandelion dreams,
Chasing shadows, lost in sunlight beams.

Her laughter floats like bubbles in the air,
A melody sweet, a moment so rare.

She's nature's retreat, wild and free,
A glowing star, a mighty sea.

She shines through storms, she soars in light,
A blazing sun, forever bright.

With each tiny step, a dance upon dew,
As the morning whispers secrets anew.

In her gaze, I find a universe wide,
Where innocence sparkles and worries subside.

Ripples

A wave of emotions crashes in,
As the summer rain begins again.

My body aches, my mind is thrown,
Into a storm of thoughts unknown.

Memories of you flood my brain,
As I'm reminded of the pain.

Of a love that once was true,
But it ended with me feeling blue.

I question why it had to end,
And wonder if I am unworthy again.

My mood swings like a hormonal pendulum,
From feeling unworthy to feeling numb.

But I know these feelings won't last,
My strength will rise, outgrow the past.

Through shifting thoughts and memories grim,
I'll find the light when days seem dim.

For I am more than just my past,
And my worth will always last.

Through the highs and through the lows,
I'll stand tall and let my confidence grow.

Soulplate

Love is a kulfi on a summer day,
Melting worries far away.
A child's delight, a joyous cheer,
As the vendor's bells ring near.

Rainy nights and pakoras hot,
Minty chutney hits the spot.
Peace is found in every bite,
A hug of warmth, pure delight.

Biryani's spice, lassi's cool,
A mix of love, a perfect rule.
Cousins fight for golgappas crisp,
A bond that's sealed with every sip.

Time drifts softly like the evening breeze,
In every moment, a sense of ease.
From bustling streets to quiet lanes,
Connection flourishes, joy remains.

Lifeline

This song of mine, so soft and light,
Will kiss your head each gentle night.
No hands will move, no words be said,
Yet love will wrap you, light as thread.

When you're alone and feeling small,
It will be near, though none may call.
And in a crowd, where you might hide,
My song will walk close by your side.

It will be wings for dreams you keep,
That lift you high while you're asleep.
It won't be loud, it won't be strong,
But it will guide your heart along.

It lives inside your tender eyes,
To help you see where beauty lies.
And though my voice may one day rest,
My love will still live in your chest.

For even when I'm gone from view,
This song will always sing in you.
A mother's love, so deep, so true,
Forever lives in all you do.

Beacon

Leaves danced under silver streams,
As if swaying in forgotten dreams.

The lightning lit up the violet skies,
Like fleeting hope in tired eyes.

With laughter echoing, memories shared,
In fleeting moments, we're all bared.

When nights are dark and skies are wide,
This will shine and be your guide.

Like stars that glow but never fall,
It will be there to hear your call.

Whispers of kinship in every glance,
A tapestry woven, given a chance.

So let the skies turn gray above,
Still it blooms in all I love.

Prajakta

I remember that first time still,
Tiny hands, a rustling thrill.

Fingers curled round fragrant stars,
Heaven, gathered in dusty jars.

The river hummed a lullaby,
The earth was wet, the sky hung low.

Yet in my palms, those blossoms glowed,
Like childhood's joy, in quiet flow.

They bloom when the world sleeps,
In monsoon hush, in autumn's breath.

She is the shy bride of night,
Whispers secrets before dawn's death.

Night jasmines, soft as clouded sighs,
Fall like dreams from darkened skies.

By morning light, they're gone from view,
Yet their perfume clings like memory's dew.

From heaven's bough, it once was torn,
By Krishna's love, to Earth it's worn.

At Rukmini's feet, the bloom was laid,
And thus, its grace on Earth has stayed.

Loop

Lost in a labyrinth of calendar invites,
Where "ASAP" means eventually tonight.
Ambitions reheated like last week's lunch,
With dreams shelved neatly by the water punch.

Polishing pitches with poetic flair,
While PowerPoint crashes mid-air.
Smiles are rehearsed, scripts on loop,
Purpose buried in the shared drive group.

Forecasts cloudy, with a chance of slides,
Yet onward we stroll, with hopeful strides.
Crafting meaning from muted calls,
Collecting courage between snack stall brawls.

Blessed with chances? Or Excel sheets?
Drowning in jargon and half-filled meets.
Should I reply-all, or quietly scream?
A soul once vibrant, now runs on memes.

Celestia

She walks through storms with silent grace,
A thousand battles on her face.
Yet still she smiles, her head held high,
A burning fire behind each eye.

She loves with depth, yet stands alone,
A heart of gold, a spine of stone.
Through every wound and every scar,
She learns to shine, just like a star.

She finds her voice in silent song,
A melody where she belongs.
And as the storm clouds fade away,
She stands unbroken, come what may.

They try to break her, dim her light,
But she was born from darkest night.
A moon in shadows, bold and bright,
She dances still, and holds on tight.

Lunar Waltz

As night grows dark, its light is shown,
A peaceful glow so softly thrown.
Behind the clouds, it hides and plays,
Yet still, its shine will find its ways.

The waves are pulled, their dance is slow,
By gentle hands they cannot know.
A quiet touch, so far yet near,
That calms the tides and holds them dear.

The breeze it carries soft perfume,
Of blooming flowers in the gloom.
Each petal sways, a silent prayer,
Embracing whispers in the air.

Its scars are made by time and past,
Yet still, its glow will always last.
Though marks remain upon its face,
Its light is full of love and grace.

Chitra

Where bamboo bows and shadows lie,
A child was born beneath a silent sky.
She bore no veil, no bashful grace,
But carved her name in battle's face.

With lifted chin and unshod feet,
She learned to fight, not to retreat.
And all who watched her blaze and burn,
Felt something shift, then twist and turn.

He came from lands the stars forgot,
A prince of dust, with battles sought.
She caught him not with smile or plea,
But with the strength of standing free.

She knelt to gods of whispered dreams,
And let her roughness split at seams.
She wore the dusk in borrowed grace,
Soft shadows brushed across her face.

In every clash, her spirit soared,
From whispered tales, her fate was forged.
With every scar, a story grew,
A tapestry of crimson and blue.

Sway

In the summer realm of June, my heart took flight,
Embarking on a journey, a traveler's delight.

The air held scents of something new,
Of freedom, of joy, of skies so blue.

Eyes wide with wonder, I chased the unknown,
Where every corner felt like home.

Each path I took, each breath of air,
Whispered stories, sacred and rare.

The cities I met held me like a song,
Filling my silence, where I'd belong.

Murals on walls, the scent of street spice,
Smiles from strangers all pure, all nice.

And as the sun dipped, painting skies with its hue,
I knew in my spirit, this journey was true.

Bayfront

"Mama, Dada, we are here again!"
I'd cry from the car, pressed to the windowpane.
"Why can't we stop? It looks so grand,
The sea, the hills, this golden land!"

And one day we did, not just pass by,
We stayed, and I felt like I could fly.
A city not just seen, but deeply felt,
Where sun-kissed shores made my heart melt.

School bells rang, college days flew,
Friends were made, and I outgrew.
The little girl who pressed the glass,
But in this city, roots grew fast.

And now I wander, but still I know,
Where the Bay of Bengal sends its glow.
For even if I roam or stray,
She lives in me, every day.

Valor

They walk not for glory, nor riches, nor fame,
But for the soil beneath their feet, they bear the flame.
Beyond the bounds of caste or creed,
They serve one flag, one sacred deed.

In shadows cast, their courage gleams,
Each heartbeat echoes with silent dreams.
They venture forth, beyond the known,
While strength at home is bravely sown.

And let us not forget the ones,
Who stay behind ,the daughters, sons,
The parents, spouses, brave and still,
Who hold the fort with iron will.

In whispered prayers, their hope endures,
In silenced rooms, their heartbeats lures.
For in each moment, bold and free,
Their legacy stretches, an endless sea.

With every dawn, their spirits rise,
A testament beneath vast skies.
In every story, their names we chant,
For freedom's call, they bravely plant.

Eclipse

That summer night was hot,
like a luscious crab in its shell,
flesh burning beneath moon's breath,
air thick with whispers and things unsaid.
We met where the tiles remembered,
our footprints pressing stories into the grout.

Your hands, cool as the grave,
found mine and
our cold-hearted warm bodies grew firm,
resurrected by want,
Soft light slid across our backs,
touching, brushing, coaxing the dead to dance.

Lips lit the unknown,
striking sparks across the void,
a map of forgotten desire,
etched in shadows and skin
tasting of pineapple - sweet and sour,
sunlit flesh and storm-swallowed regrets.

We were fools then,
laughing loud into the silence,
alive again in that glimmering edge
between memory and midnight.
The hallway mirrors caught us
reflection of reflections,
gleaming truths with no past.

There, we glowed.
There, we made the pact
to meet each year,
on the hottest night,
where the air still touches,
and the dead still crave
to feel their bodies again.

Haven

The full moon bathed the sea in light,
Silver waves danced through the night.

While new moon skies turned deep and black,
The quiet tide still called us back.

The breeze would hush the crowded mind,
And leave the weight of days behind.

Each tide would bring a lullaby,
That rose and fell beneath the sky.

Laughter echoed in our halls,
Between the drips on windowed walls.

No riches shone, yet joy would stay,
In every salt-soaked, wind-blown day.

Humidity clung, both bold and true,
But hearts stayed light beneath that hue.

No skyline vast, no bustling spree,
Just small town calm and endless sea.

For home was more than roof or land,
It lived where sea and soul would stand.

And in that breeze, so wild and free,
We found our world beside the sea.

Opaque

A friend to all is a friend to none,
Amidst a crowd, in distant lands.
Toiling hard, with no team in sight,
A solitary soul, navigating the night.

Laughs echo, smiles adorn the face,
Yet within, a vacant, silent space.
Helping others, organizing the show,
In a room full of people, lost in the flow.

Events unfold, activities engage,
A tireless spirit on life's stage.
Fatigue sets in, yet sleep eludes,
In solitude, where silence intrudes.

The heart aches for a taste of true bond,
A flicker of warmth in the vast beyond.
Seeking a kindred spirit to share,
To break the spell of this empty air.

Plink

The skies went grey, a hush in the air,
A cool breeze danced through my open hair.
The heat gave in, the world stood still,
As clouds rolled in over the silent hill.

A sudden flash, a roaring sound,
Thunder echoed, shaking the ground.
I held my breath, heart skipping a beat,
Yet smiled as the rain began its gentle feat.

Petrichor rose from the thirsty land,
Like nature's perfume, subtle and grand.
Each drop a kiss, so soft, so true,
Painting the earth in a glistening hue.

I watched it all from my little nook,
With a steaming cup and a half-read book.
The world outside in a watery haze,
Wrapped me in its monsoon embrace.

Nimbu Paani

We sit on rooftops counting stars,
Long drives, short naps in shaded cars.
The sun may scorch, but we don't mind,
It burns in ways that feel so kind.

Vacations stretch like endless days,
No school bells ring, no rigid ways.
We visit cousins, laugh and roam,
In grandma's arms, we find our home.

Afternoons blaze with silent heat,
Yet every evening feels like a treat.
Cool breeze, a mat, a glass in hand,
With stories shared just as we planned.

To scents, to sounds, to skies so wide,
Where laughter, love, and time reside.
Oh summer, stay in heart and hue,
A season lived, forever new.

Angry Bird

Blue skies call me to wander far,
Summer sunsets trace where memories are.

Mint lemonades in mason jars,
And laughter under scattered stars.

Winter wraps me in silent grace,
Dark nights, warm lights, your sweet embrace.

Fireplaces hum our quiet song,
In your arms is where I belong.

Grilled cheese kisses on cozy days,
Hazelnut coffee in sunlit cafés.

Macarons, moments, a chocolate delight,
You make even stormy days feel light.

Slow trains pass, I gaze through mist,
Each photograph a moment kissed.

Every distant view I chase,
Leads me back to your quiet grace.

Over all the things I love and know,
Over places I've been, the paths I go.

With your furrowed brows and heart of gold
Grumbling at the world, yet soft with me,
You're the calm, the storm, my melody.

Coach

Rattling tracks and rhythmic chug,
It's path is a no mere hug.
From the hills to the sea,
A unique experience for you and me.

Friendly faces and endless smiles,
Traveling a journey of miles.
The sound of vendors with their wares,
Selling little ornaments, snacks, and pillows.

The rhythmic clatter on the track,
A gentle sway, there's no turning back.
Each passing scene, a brand new sight,
Bathed in the soft and silvery light.

The Sun and the stars are its only guide,
And the wind is the only song beside.
So relax, and enjoy the ride,
Through the plains and the countryside.

Across the land of vibrant hues,
Where stories flow and dreams infuse.
From bustling cities to fields so green,
An Indian train, a captivating scene.

Sepia

In narrow lanes where marbles rolled,
And secret crushes shyly told.

With Walkmans on and tapes rewind,
Our hearts began to gently bind.

Sharing Frooti on a summer day,
Stealing glances, then looking away.

In sticker books and school bus rides,
Young love bloomed where joy resides.

Pencil shavings, slam book names,
Silly jokes and playful games.

Friendship bands on August days,
Tied with hopes in childish ways.

Sunday mornings, cartoons on loop,
Bicycle rides with the neighborhood group.

Tazos traded, candies shared,
A world so small, yet deeply cared.

Old school days, so pure, so deep,
It visits still in midnight sleep.

A story written, soft and slow,
In every heart that used to glow.

Velvet

In a bustling city where moments flew,
A soul was found, unexpected and new.
A jack of all trades, with stories untold,
He spoke of places and things so bold.

Through crowded streets and city sound,
Steps wandered where new tastes are found.
A drive in café, quiet and small,
Held a drink that would change it all.

The first sip, a gentle surprise,
Chewy bubbles, a soft reprise.
Sticky and sweet, they danced within,
A joy that lingered, deep within.

The liquid swirled with flavors so true,
The pearls, like jewels, a perfect hue.
Black and brown, they softly gleamed,
Like treasures from a dream that beamed.

In that moment, nothing was rushed,
Each sip, each bubble, the taste was lush.
A feeling was savored, so complete,
In the quiet pleasure of Boba tea's sweet.

Gleam

The cold nights stretch out so long,
And chimney fires burn bright and strong.
Their smoke drifts up to stormy skies,
As darkness falls before my eyes.

I sit and watch the stars align,
A peaceful, quiet, gentle sign.
The wild sea breeze, so crisp and cool,
Touches my skin, by window rule.

An owl's soft cry within the night,
Echoes through darkness, sifting light.
Up stairs I walk, with quiet pace,
To see the twilight's misty face.

The moon shines through the clouds above,
A glimmering sign of lasting love.
And in that moment, clear and true,
I think of winters spent with you.

With every sigh the night bestows,
I weave your memory, soft it glows.
The whispers of the past still linger,
In shadows cast by fire's finger.

Tide Folk

Before the dawn, when skies are gray,
They rise and make their way.
With hearts so brave, and hands so strong,
They sail the seas where they belong.

The boats set sail, the nets are cast,
Through waves and winds, they journey fast.
Their skin may burn, their hearts may ache,
But for their families, they will not break.

The sea, their mistress, wild and free,
They know her whispers, her dark decree.
They speak her language, and learn her ways,
Each morning, each night, through endless days.

They dive and swim in ocean's blue,
Chasing the fish that dart and move.
With steady hands, they pull them near,
A feast for loved ones, year by year.

Each night they pray, with hearts aglow,
To the sea deity for the winds to slow.
A life of toil, of love, of grace,
The fishermen, heroes of the sea's embrace.

Muselet

She clocks in after nine, her game face on,
Through deadlines and calls, she powers strong.

Yet behind the poise, the grace she hid,
Lies laughter unfiltered yes, she's still a kid.

She trades weekends for college halls,
Chasing dreams, answering distant calls.

Juggling life, making every end meet,
Yet her joy is found in the simplest treat.

She's no more a child, yet more than she seems,
A master of tasks, a weaver of dreams.

A tapestry woven with threads of her might,
She dances through shadows, embracing the light.

A daughter so dutiful, with hands that heal,
A woman of beauty, strength, and zeal.

Thaal

Where Deccan's sun-kissed stones ascend,
And winds whisper scents that flavors send.

A ruby drink, Solkadhi's cool caress,
Vada Pav's spice in humble excess.

Pav Bhaji's vibrant, joyful flair,
And Pithala Bhakri's love, beyond compare.

Like sago pearls, Sabudana Vadi gleam,
Beside Kotimbir Vadi's fragrant dream.

Thali Peeth's layers, rustic and whole,
Misal Pav's fire, ignites the soul.

Steamed Modak, a cherished sweet,
A taste of home in every bite we meet.

Puran Poli's golden, soft embrace,
A comforting joy beneath the sky's grace.

Bharl Vangi's spice, an adventure begun,
Shrikhand's silk, a creamy, cooling sun.

Each taste a journey, genuine and true,
A personalized joy, crafted for you.

Whispers of fragrance, upon the breeze,
Amid the swaying, ancient tamarind trees.

Evermore

She'll immortalize your eyes so deep,
In pages where her secrets sleep.
She won't intrude, nor claim your space,
Yet loves you with a boundless grace.

She'll trace your past in tender lines,
Turn pain to prose, let love define.
Her words will dance, a whispered art,
That softens even the coldest heart.

She holds her head with quiet pride,
With dignity she steps aside.
She'll weave your name in midnight air,
Yet walk alone without despair.

And one day when the echoes grow,
You'll hear her voice in winds that blow.
Regret may come, but time won't bend,
For she stood strong, yet loved till end.

Pahari

Suddenly, before me, a sight so grand,
A vast expanse, where earth meets sky, unplanned.
From the wing, the world unfurled,
With peaks rising sharp, like an ancient world.

A horizon of jagged giants, so bold,
Their snow-covered faces, stories untold.
Each one distinct, a silhouette clear,
Bathed in light and shadow, drawing near.

Each Himalayan peak, a name known to the brave,
A beauty eternal, impossible to cage.
The scene sways, a dynamic breath,
Alive in its grandeur, defying death.

Each crevice, a secret, each valley, a tale,
Of journeys uncharted, of dreams that unveil.
It looks like a painting, tender and true,
Snow and shadows in a painter's hue.

With brush in hand, I long to capture,
This wildness ,its power, its fractured rapture.
For in this grand vision, transient and vast,
Lives a memory kindled, a love that will last.

Blurred

With a camera in hand, I wander wide,
Capturing moments with stories inside.
I snap the shutter, time stands still,
Preserving memories with every skill.

Yet no one asks to be in my frame,
No one longs to share my name.
I flip through shots and wonder why,
Is it the fear of being seen by an eye?

Still, I feel a little alone,
Capturing scenes not truly my own.
I wish for once they'd call me near,
To be in the frame, to stand sincere.

But as I ponder on this thought,
I realize something I once forgot.
I came to find the beauty untold,
Even if I remain unseen and cold.

Though I may not be in sight,
I'm part of the story, bathed in light.
So I'll keep clicking, capturing the scene,
A silent observer to a world serene.

Sweet Creature

In love's pursuit, beyond the limits I danced,
Life's a sweet jest and serenade enhanced.
Yet, the laughter unveiled a bittersweet truth,
Reached destinations, yet missed you, in sooth.

You gathered blossoms, filled your embrace,
I stayed behind, a flower, in love's grace.
Dreams linger in my gaze, a vivid sight,
Moments turned into memories, soft and bright.

Where are you now, in this city of dreams?
My heart seeks you in the moon's soft beams.
Unseen, you linger, lost in the maze,
Silent echoes, where love's essence stays.

In time's tapestry, a thread left astray,
A puzzle unsolved, in my heart's array.
Yet, in silence, your essence I savor,
Love's melody, an eternal flavor.

Jatraa

Not carved with gold, nor crowned in flame,
But sindoor-smeared, in simple frame.

A stone divine, yet strong and deep,
She guards the city while it sleeps.

Like children drawn to mother's grace,
We find our calm in her embrace.

She is our protector, our shield,
Before her might, the darkest yields.

The lanes awake with sound and shade,
In colors loud, the vows are made.

Giant Raths, mythic and grand,
Roll through the dust, across the land.

Veshas bloom in vibrant art,
Each form a prayer, a beating heart.

The drums, the chants, the flickered lights,
Breathe life into the sacred nights.

She walks the town in every face,
In every dance, in every grace.

She blesses all, both old and new,
With mother's love, so fierce and true.

Spectrum

There are truths that cannot be seen,
Hidden beyond what eyes have gleaned,
Yet without a blink, you stand untold,
A timeless beauty, silent and bold.

A pearl within an ocean's heart,
Waiting, pure, for dreams to start.
Like rainbows spread on fabric bright,
You are the soul of joy and light.

Your words are crafted, sharp and wise,
A pair that dazzles, and defies.
Yet still, you stand with quiet might,
A stop sign in the endless night.

Let your fantasy rise and fly,
Like colors bursting in the sky.
In silence, beauty finds its place,
In stillness, love unveils its face.

Kaveri

I walked the path, my steps unsure,
The river whispered allure.

The air was thick, with mist and sound,
I had no idea what I had just found.

The water crashed, tumbling from heights,
Like a thousand spirits taking flight.

It roared with power, fierce and free,
A symphony of life, wild and endless, you see.

The birds above in perfect flight,
Seemed to dive into the misty light.

Each droplet a mirror, a tale to unfold,
Of dreams carried softly, of secrets retold.

The river's force, the waterfall's might,
Shone in the day, and glowed at night.

The sound was beyond belief,
A hush of nature, yet strong like a thief.

Her waters carried the weight of the past,
And in her roar, I was free at last.

Mishti

Her stories flow like rivers wide,
Tales of her youth and the times she'd bide.

Of traditions old, and songs so sweet,
Of memories shared, where hearts meet.

Her kitchen hums with magic's tune,
Her pickles, sweets, they make us swoon.

Achar so spicy, and treats divine,
Each bite a memory, each dish a sign.

Though recipes passed through years of time,
The taste of her hands is simply sublime.

No matter the effort, no matter the try,
Her cooking is the taste we can't deny.

The secret's not in the spice or flame,
It's the love in her heart, the warmth in her name.

A grandmother's hands, so skilled, so true,
Create a world where dreams come through.

She is the epitome of love and grace,
A timeless soul, in every embrace.

Her legacy lives, in each dish she makes,
In every smile, in every heart that breaks.

For in her, we find the world's true light,
The wisdom, the love, the sweet delight.

A grandmother's touch is forever dear,
A treasure to hold, year after year.

Zest

A season kissed by Mango light,
Where mornings bloom, and hearts feel right.
Plums and lychees, their scent so sweet,
Dripping joy in every treat.

Watermelon - crimson, cold and wide,
A juicy hug on the hottest side.
Chiku's charm, so soft and mild,
Ice apple cools the sunburnt child.

Water apple with a pinkish glow,
Refreshes souls that summers know.
Jamun stains both lips and tongue,
With purple song of summers sung.

Starfruit arcs in crystal sprays,
Scattering magic through the days.
Oh, the golden days of May's grace,
With sunshine dancing on every face.

Shield

At Siachen's frost, where breath runs thin,
They hold their post through ice and wind.
Where Rajasthan's deserts fiercely blaze,
They guard the sands through scorching days.

By the Line of Control, sharp and steep,
They brave the dark, while we all sleep.
By Assam's jungles, wet and wild,
They march through storms, terrain defiled.

Down to the Southern seas so vast,
They shield our shores from threats that pass.
In Punjab's fields, in Bengal's plains,
In sun or flood, in drought or rains.

For every corner, they take their stand,
In whispered winds, a silent band.
With hearts of steel, and spirits bright,
They face the dawn, embracing the fight.

Chenna Poda

Cheese, sugar, semolina's grace,
Pressed with care, in an earthen place.
Cardamom sang, cashews curled,
And Odisha's magic slowly swirled.

Caramel kissed its surface deep,
A secret the fire was meant to keep.
Schoolbag hung, the day still warm,
I saw it nestled in Dad's palm.

He smiled and said, "Taste this once,"
His eyes lit up like monsoon suns.
One bite in, and time stood still,
The crust, the melt, the sugar thrill.

Not cake, not fudge, not bread, not pie,
It was something words could not deny.
Soft and smoky, rich and bold,
A flavor wrapped in love and gold.

Marigold

A morning's hush, a soft hello,
The first sweet sip of golden glow.
It weaves through dawn in threads of grace,
And wraps the sky in warm embrace.

It blooms in fields where sunflowers sway,
Their golden faces greet the day.
In daffodils that laugh in tune,
Beneath the kiss of early June.

It stains my palms like turmeric's hue,
A mark of all that's pure and true.
It dances in the fire's low gleam,
A candle's flicker, soft as dream.

It's warmth that stays through cold and fear,
The light I hold when none is near.
It rests in sunsets, bold and bright,
And rises slow with morning light.

Wayfarer

Bags were packed, and steps were led,
By whispers of dreams softly spread.
Paths unfolded without a plan,
As time slipped gently from the span.

A smile was shared without a name,
A quiet joy without acclaim.
Sunrise watched with silent awe,
In places eyes had never saw.

The breeze had brushed the tired skin,
And peace was found somewhere within.
Laughter echoed, stories grew,
Not from things, but moments true.

Sunsets caught from random bends,
Stories birthed, where journey mends.
Not in snapshots, nor in tags,
But in the joy that memory drags.

November

A change so soft, it gently flows,
Like tender whispers that love bestows.
The air, a lover's warm embrace,
Caresses me with gentle grace.

Red, pale, blue, and pink above,
The sky, a canvas, gentle love.
Not cold, nor dry, it held me close,
In shifting hues, I found repose.

The trees stand bare, yet full of grace,
Their branches etched in time and space.
Leaves, once golden, now drift away,
As autumn whispers its last display.

The earth wears a blanket, soft and deep,
A quiet hush where shadows sleep.
The sky, a canvas brushed in gold,
Tells stories of the young and old.

Memories lingered, clear and bright,
Haunting whispers through the night.
I tried to hold them, tried to stay,
But change kept calling, led the way.

Zenith

Creative minds and bold debates,
Where words flow free, no fears, no weights.

Winter evenings, soft and clear,
Wrapped in warmth, the ones I hold dear.

Kindness flows like a gentle stream,
Gratitude weaves through every dream.

Art in whispers, strokes on days,
Blissful sunsets, in golden rays.

Long drives with the wind in my hair,
Vintage diaries, moments to share.

Slow dance arms, a gentle sway,
Under the moonlight, we drift away.

Music hums as the stars align,
Forehead kisses, soft and divine.

Simple texts that make me smile,
Endless imaginations running wild.

In every little thing, joy lights the way,
Gratitude grows with each new day.

With every heartbeat, with every smile,
Positive vibes that make life worthwhile.

Laboratory

Graduation neared like dusk to day,
While others packed and walked away.
Pipettes, beakers, the scent of flame,
In that sacred lab, I found my name.

I lingered there with stubborn pride,
Argued with ma'am, stayed by her side.
She'd sigh, "It's time," I'd still resist,
As if the lab would cease to exist.

Experiments whispered like old friends,
Unwritten stories without ends.
But medals rust, and time moves on,
And I now walk a different dawn.

I have grown, and life has too,
The path I walk is noble, true.
But Ten percent of me still yearns,
For agar plates and Bunsen burns.

And though regret is faint and light,
A shadow cast by love and might.
It's not a wound, but just a trace,
Of where my heart once found its place.

Trishanvi

They told me, "Child, he has no name.
He wears no pride, he holds no fame.

His throne's a rock, his robe is skin,
He dances wild with ghosts and sin.

Why seek a man who shuns the skies?
You were born for kings to idolize."

But true love knows not of gold,
It blooms where stories go untold.

I saw not ash, but purest flame,
I saw the soul, not world-built name.

He was the truth the world denies,
The stillness deep where silence lies.

So to the woods I walked, alone,
With every step, shed flesh and throne.

I learned the wind, I spoke to stone,
I let the forest make me known.

I am stillness in the flame,
The shadow that will always remain.

For years I prayed beneath the pine,
Till even the cold stars saw me shine.

Visakha

Evenings drifted on beachside walks,
Where silver waves hummed quiet talks.
Bheemili sands beneath our feet,
With wind-blown hair and hearts that beat,

RK beach's golden sprawl,
Where laughter echoed, free for all.
Ice creams melted in salty air,
And movie nights at Jagadamba Square,

From Kailasagiri's winding rail,
To Araku's misty morning trail,
Coffee farms and silent trees,
Valleys carved by gentle breeze,

Steel plant's lights, the old sweet shops,
Evening chats at roadside stops.
City buses with seaside views,
And secret spots we'd always choose.

Now miles away, I close my eyes,
And see those hills, those ocean skies.
Each street, each turn, a memory spun,
Of all we were when we were young.

Tether

In the heart of a boy, the only star of his skies,
Loved by a girl with wonder in her eyes.

Their joy runs deep, a bond truly grown,
Yet in quiet hours, he feels all alone.

Uncertainty lingers, with storms held inside,
A tangle of truths he struggles to hide.

Wading through sarcasm, drifting in streams,
Caught in a world of fragmented dreams.

He stands at the brink of a future unknown,
A path untraveled, he must walk alone.

But love is his compass, his anchor, his guide,
A light in the dark when hope wants to hide.

Strings

There's a silence that sings within me,
Not of absence, but of dreams unsaid,
Where melodies drift, soft and unshed,
Like whispers shaped by winds instead.

The stage - my dream, my distant shore,
A world I've watched but not explored.
Not for lack of love or fire,
But paths that pulled me from desire.

The strings that hum, the keys that chime,
Each note a balm, each beat in time.
The veena sings, the guitar weeps,
And in that tune, my spirit leaps.

When shadows stretch and spirits fade,
It soothes the soul, a serenade.
No temple walls or sacred shrine,
Just sound that lifts, a force divine,

It lives in me, not just in song,
A quiet flame that burns lifelong.
Though stage and spotlight pass me by,
Its echo stays, it will not die.

Chimera

Each night I slip to fractured land,
Where logic slips from trembling hand.

A masquerade of smoke and shade,
Where faces twist and truths degrade,
And sanity begins to strand.

I chase, I'm chased, the blood runs wild,
One moment killer, next a child.

I see my end, then rise once more,
Through dreamscapes drenched in mental gore,
Each heartbeat loud and unreconciled.

The sleep I seek does not arrive,
I lie too still, yet feel alive.

The mind ignites, the reel begins,
Insomnia crawls beneath my skin.
And morning finds me half-survived.

So they twist through every mind,
A hidden world, unbound, unkind.

They steal our rest, distort our view,
Leave echoes we can't quite undo,
A silent storm that no one outruns.

Timberline

It was said
a tree once grew in the middle of wind.
Not in soil,
but in the breath between two forgotten names.

No seed was seen falling.
No roots were mapped.
Yet there it was
unmoved,
even when the sky peeled open
and flung its fists across the earth.

Storms arrived wearing masks of water and rage.
The birds fled.
The fields unstitched themselves.
But the tree
it bent without breaking,
spoke in the rustle of resistance,
and let the cyclone scream through its silence.

They say the air around it felt clearer.
People didn't see it
but their lungs remembered.
Children played in its shadow without knowing
they were being kept.

It gave without giving
oxygen, shade, a place for tired wings.
No applause was heard.
No thank-you carved.
But dust fell softer where it stood.

Now it's said
that if you pass the place between the winds,
you might not see the tree.
But the silence there is shaped
like something that once stood
and never asked to be known.

Jishnu

He turned, bounded by scented air,
By moonlit skin and loosened hair.

But when the drums of danger rolled,
She rose as flame no charm could hold.

And he, once drawn to lips and lace,
Now saw the truth behind the face.

He loved her not for what she'd feigned,
But for the fire she had retained.

For she was fern, and she was flame,
And he, the one who knew her name.

Not just the hush, but every cry,
The storm beneath the summer sky.

In Chitra's eyes, he found a grace,
Not draped in silk, but battle's face.

Their love was quiet, strong, and wide,
Two kindred flames that walked side by side.

Through tempest winds and shadows cast,
Their souls entwined, forever fast.

In every heartbeat, every sigh,
The world would fade as they would fly.

Undertow

Bare feet sink into velvet sand,
As foamy kisses greet the land.
Each wave, a milk-white, frothing sigh,
That dances low, then soars up high.

They come and go in timeless grace,
A tender, ageless, sweet embrace.
Where rhythm meets the yearning tide,
And soul and sea are unified.

The burdens borne by weary feet,
Were loosened where the waters meet.
Beneath the waves, soft sorrows sleep,
In cradle sways, the oceans keep.

Each ache is brushed by salt and sigh,
Then lulled beneath the open sky.
Popsicles melted on unseen hands,
As laughter slipped like silver sands.

A wish was breathed that time might cease,
And life be held in endless peace.
Where never-ending waves were seen,
And souls could rest within a dream.

Glimmer

Let puddles call you now and then,
Draw silly doodles with your pen.

Sing off-key, and laugh too loud,
Run barefoot, break free from the crowd.

A candy split, a giggle shared,
No grand displays, just souls that cared,

No screens, no noise ,just quiet grace,
And love that time could not erase.

So wear your worries like paper hats,
Spin in circles, talk to cats.

Chase butterflies, chase fleeting dreams,
Dance in the rain, let it burst at the seams.

In whispered secrets beneath the stars,
Find magic tucked in a jar of jars.

Share secrets sweet as summer's breeze,
Collect memories like autumn leaves.

So laugh like the world is yours to make,
And find the beauty in every mistake.

Let wonder in, let joy run wild,
Grow wise, but keep the heart of a child.

Uma

He tested me, in rage and fire,
He hid his face, suppressed desire.

Among the peaks, beneath the sky,
We wed with wind and stars nearby.

I was no more a queen of land,
But the bride who chose his wandering hand.

They call it madness. I call it grace.
To love the soul, not just the face.

To walk through fire, and choose the flame,
To lose the world, yet earn a name.

He spoke in silence, deep and wide,
The mountains moved, the oceans sighed.

For in his arms, I found the whole,
A home, a world, a mirror, a soul.

For even storm and tempest's might
Can't dim the bond we forged in light.

With every breath, the cosmos spun,
A tapestry of two as one.

Mizzle

And just as the monsoon kissed the land,
Raindrops danced like a painter's hand.

Washing the dust, the noise, the rush
The world stood still in a sacred hush.

The days of toil, the routine grind,
Faded behind as I realigned.

The world outside in stillness lies,
Reflecting stars in frosty skies,

A quiet peace that never dies,
Within this sweet surprise.

With every droplet, whispers call,
In nature's arms, I grew so small.

The trees, a chorus, sing so bright,
Guiding lost souls back to the light.

And in their shade, I learned to play,
To dance through life in a kinder way.

For every storm that sweeps the sea
Brings forth the blooms that set us free.

Tropica

Scarves wrapped tight, a sunlit veil,
As we walk through noon's blazing trail.

Sunscreen lingers on every skin,
A battle won before we begin.

Footprints dance on warm, sandy shores,
Echoing dreams as the ocean roars.

Evenings glow with a breezy cheer,
As chilled drinks and laughter draw near.

The night wraps us in its silken thread,
While fireflies flicker, softly we tread.

Memories linger in twilight's hue,
A canvas of moments, forever new.

A time that sings, a time that stays,
Forever locked in golden days.

Mellowdust

QWERTY keys, we typed with care,
Saving texts that felt so rare.
A hundred messages meant the most,
Each one treasured like a toast.

TV time with family near,
Sundays filled with cheer and gear.
Swinging high beneath the trees,
Collecting stamps and memories.

Diaries locked with little keys,
Secret crushes, scraped-up knees.
Playgrounds roared with hide and seek,
Life was magic, wild and meek.

Wishes whispered on dandelion puffs,
Braving the world, we were bold, we were tough.
Friendship bracelets, woven tight,
Promises made under the soft starlight.

Time flowed by, a gentle stream,
Holding close each fleeting dream.
Yet here we stand, hearts still free,
Forever bound by memory.

21

Self-worth was questioned in tired reflections,
and dreams were doubted under city lights.

The silly dances, the endless giggles,
the wild, reckless hopes ,all were quietly abandoned,
packed away like old toys in dusty corners of the mind.
The foolish bravery that once wore scraped knees
proudly
was traded for careful silences and hidden scars.

The wide-eyed wonder was replaced
by measured glancces and cautious steps.

Slowly, the world demanded the magic to be unlearned,
the innocence to be unstitched,
and the softest parts of the heart
to be tucked away
for the sake of survival.

Yet somewhere, amidst the chaos,

small victories were celebrated in whispered pride.

Love for fleeting moments was relearned,
kindness was pulled from buried places,
and strength was stitched together from broken dreams.

Stillness

It looks like a painting, tender and true,
Snow and shadows in a painter's hue.
With brush in hand, I long to capture,
This wildness- its power, its fractured rapture.

The terrain is rugged, raw, and wild,
A landscape both fierce and mild.
The sun dips low, a fiery farewell,
Casting spells where the shadows dwell.

Snow lays thick, both dark and bright,
As edges and ridges come to life in light.
I thought of those who scale these heights,
Risking all to challenge the nights.

Above the clouds, in crisp, clear air,
They glimpse the world, untouched and rare.
Their journey etched in ice and stone,
Their courage is seen in the unknown.

Hush

The trees stand bare, yet full of grace,
Their branches etched in time and space.
Leaves, once golden, now drift away,
As autumn whispers its last display.

Each crackling leaf a tale to tell,
Of fleeting days that once rang bright and well.
The coldness lingers in the air,
But love is felt in moments rare.

Soft whispers travel through the trees,
As hearts are stirred by gentle breeze.
The northern winds still softly sigh,
Yet golden rays now warm the sky.

The trees may stand in stark display,
Yet hope prevails in night's soft sway.
The frost that once had ruled the land,
Now yields beneath the sun's command.

Savour

On streets bustling, flavors collide,
Chaat and biryani, a savory ride.
Rosogolla soft, Vadapav bold,
Sweet and spice, a story told.

Adventure waits in hills so high,
With Wai-Wai crisp beneath the sky.
Dosa golden, sambhar flows,
Like a love that always grows.

Every dish, a tale so true,
Food is love, in taste and hue.
From every state, a flavor divine,
A plate of joy, a love that shines.

Each meal shared, a bond so tight,
In kitchens and hearts, the love ignites.
So let us savor this rich array,
In every morsel, love finds its way.

Nocturne

A weary heart is wrapped in peace,
As softest beams bring quiet ease.
No words are heard, yet souls are healed,
By gentle light that stays concealed.

Each dawn awakens dreams anew,
As hope begins to pierce the blue.
And as the night fades into day,
Its soothing glow won't drift away.

For in the hearts that watch it rise,
A peaceful hush forever lies.
More than a blossom in a vase,
You paint the sky with cosmic grace.

Through every shadow, every fear,
Your light will guide us, always near.
Stars scatter, drawn by your glow,
A wonder only few may know.

Phase

With courage beneath his rising tide,
He steps into fear, with love at his side.

For even the night can't dim love's light,
It carries him through with silent might.

So he'll carve his way, with steady pace,
Through woven webs and time's embrace.

For deep in his heart, one truth ignites,
In love that is pure, burn guiding lights.

Through the confusion, he'll find her stride,
With a wink and a grin, he's in for the ride.

Inglorious shadows may come to intrude,
But kindness will echo, transforming the rude.

For in every moment, through thick and through thin,
Love's a wild adventure where every day begins!

Grind

Promised a ladder, got a swivel chair,
Climbing in circles, getting nowhere.
Direction's a myth, the path's a blur,
Each "ping" a whisper from chaos, sir.

Moments of laughter, brief sparks of gold,
In between meetings, our stories unfold.
Let's toast to the chaos, the humor we find,
In this corporate circus, we're all intertwined.

Chasing deadlines like shadows in flight,
While passion fades under fluorescent light.
Yet still we gather, woven by strife,
In this office maze, echoes of life.

Through the hustle and bustle, together we stand,
Finding solace in chaos, hand in hand.
For every misstep, a lesson we glean,
In this tangled web, we carve out our scene.

Tinker Joy

Remember the days of skinned knees,
Of chasing clouds and catching fireflies?
When the world was wide, and dreams ran wild,
In the fearless heart of a little child.

We spoke to stars, we danced with rain,
Built castles high and felt no pain.
Our pockets full of stones and songs,
In that small world where we belonged.

Then time, with quiet, hurried feet,
Led us to desks and city streets.
We learned to trade our toys for plans,
And folded dreams in grown-up hands.

But oh if you close your eyes tonight,
You'll feel that child, soft and bright.
Still laughing, still dreaming, still running free,
A version of you you're meant to be.

So gather the stardust, collect the light,
Let early dawn guide you, shining bright.
For the journey's not over, it's only begun,
Embrace that child, let your heart outrun.

Solace

The tassel was turned,
and the hands of time were unknowingly pushed
forward.

Dreams once painted in bright hues
were slowly shaded by bills, deadlines, and silent
commutes.

The soft embrace of mother's meals was replaced
by hurried dinners and lonely coffee cups.

A mind once carefree was weighed down
with silent calculations and late-night worries.

Friendships were thinned out like old letters,
as schedules were filled and promises were postponed.

Loneliness was embraced in quiet apartments,
and sleep was bargained like a luxury good.

In the mirror, a child was slowly replaced
by someone unfamiliar yet quietly resilient
for against all odds,
life was being lived,
even if some pieces had been left behind forever.

Shoulders

She twirled into his silent world,
Like sunshine through a cloudy swirl,
A tiny hand in his so wide,
A piece of heaven by his side.

Her giggles are his favorite tune,
Her sleepy eyes, a silver moon.
Each messy braid, each playful sigh,
Brings tears of joy he can't deny.

He built her swings and taught her dreams,
Fixed broken toys and sewed loose seams.
Proud smiles were worn through every grade,
As dreams and plans were gently laid.

Bags were packed with hope and grace,
Her laughter left a quiet space.
A door was closed, a car was waved,
A thousand memories silently saved.

He smiles, though silence fills the room,
Her laughter fades, replaced by gloom.
Yet in his heart, she's just the same,
His little girl, with Daddy's name.